YOU ARE NOT DEAD

A GUIDE TO MODERN LIVING

A Self Work Product from
the Fakeproject Corporation of America

Meg Holle and Daniel Reetz

🍁 Canadian Edition

This is a work about you. Faults, foolish notions, hopes, dreams, dares, schemes, scenarios and severances are either products of your own life or are used predictively. Any resemblance to you—living, dead or not dead—is entirely probable.

Published by the Author is Dead
theauthorisdead.com

The Fakeproject Corporation of America released the music, image and text collaboration *You Are Not Dead: a Guide to Modern Living* online in 2008. We thank the Canadian Chapter and Black Pants for their enthusiasm and support in creating the Canadian Edition, a significant revision of the original.

ISBN-10: 0982751303
ISBN-13: 9780982751305

For more guidance, please visit:

fakeproject.com – Fakeproject Corporation of America
youarenotdead.ca – the Canadian Chapter okayness seminar
deepsicks.com – Meg Holle's corpus
danreetz.com – Daniel Reetz's genius
blackpants.ca – Black Pants Productions

YOU ARE NOT DEAD

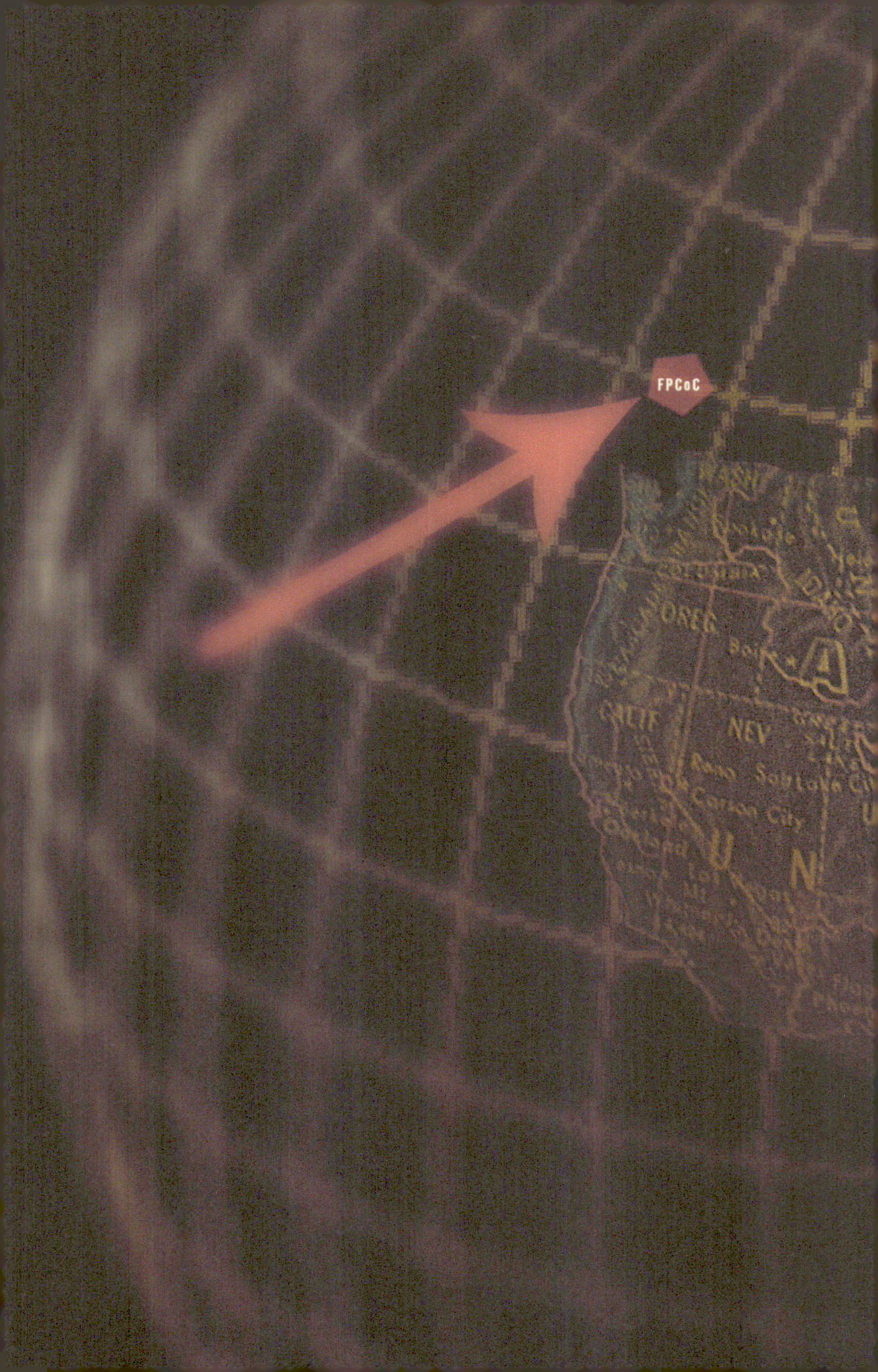
FPCoC
OREG
CALIF
NEV
Reno
Carson City

WELCOME!

You have been waiting for you! Fraught and unsteady, you're still ready to probe:

- ☑ To seek better living through not dying.
- ☑ To overcome strife and not die trying.
- ☑ To confront the patterns, dreams and dangerous notions that prevent you from fulfilling our goals.

By reading this introduction, you have reached your conclusion: a planned life beats an impulsive death, and being Not Dead trumps both.

The Fakeproject Corporation understands this, even if you don't. Associates to the south are known around the globe for managling natural resources, energy, enemies and nations, while the proud and able Canadian Chapter has long foiled behind the scenes helping keep the peaces.

But over the past few years, it has become clear to dear leadership far and wide: we cannot care nor dare for the world when the hearth goes awry. You are not dead—and you live in the best place on earth.

Yet you are barely happy.

You are hardly even here.

Working with a series of surveys, receipts and long-term surveillance, our behavioral experts and social analysts have dedicated countless hours of study to the life- and deathstyles of people like you. Research indicates patterns. Patterns improve predictably. And as statistics can be shown, our programming proves your worth in helping us help you temper your aimless movement.

Life takes work. Death takes self. Being Not Dead takes Self Work: reflective examination, self interrogation and the guts to gash the bites and suck out the poison—all your conflicting thoughts and uncooperative emotions. To encourage your progress, throughout this experience your input will be prompted. Be honest. Be bold. Check your feelings and fill in your blanks.

With the direction and determination of *You Are Not Dead: a Guide to Modern Living*, you will learn to resist trifling complexities. You will recognize the paths that are deceptively easy and those unnecessarily hard. At last you will be mindful of delusion and mean to do something about it. You will be open to closure and sew the wounds shut.

Don't fear failure nor fret stress. Thanks to careful plotting, everyone fits, and your transition will be seamless.

No more worry. No more wonder.

Let your life unfold behind you.

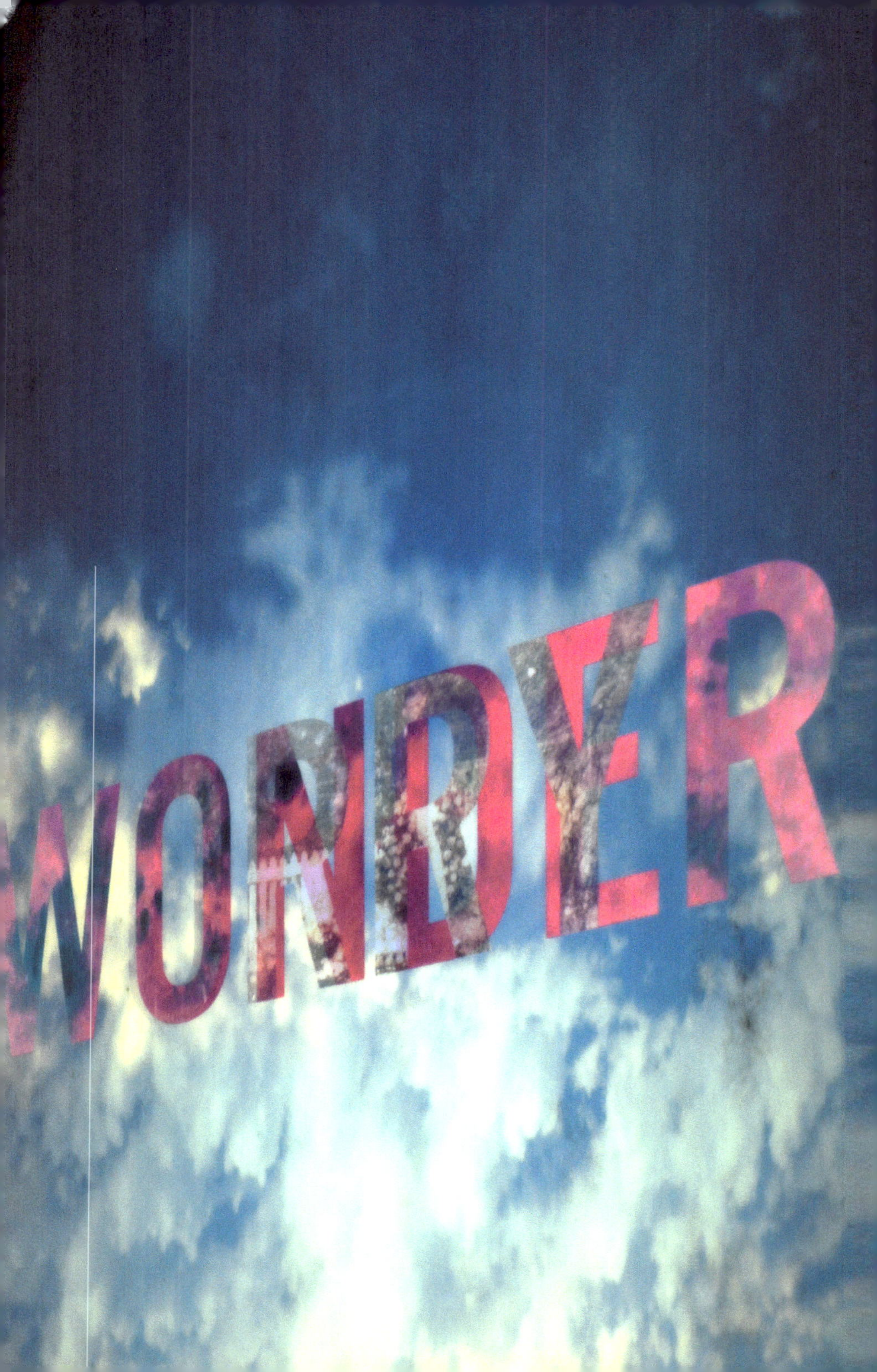

1. Getting Out of Life A̶l̶i̶v̶e̶ Not Dead

You have reached an impassive!
You cannot proceed and you are not sure you want to!
You are between a rock and a hard place!
The world and what it demands of you!

Where do you start? What should you start, and how? Where have you been, where are you now and where do you want to be?

In the present world of expectations and disappointment, hidden threats and clear danger, there are many ways to die, not the least of which is consciously—choosing death over life or surrendering in full consciousness and potential.

You, however, are Not Dead. You are among the survivors, a quick study, awake and sturdy, an able individual who knows when to follow and when to fall behind. Neither solider nor stranger to structured living, you play the game well, even if it disgusts you— trusting to be trusted, serving to be served, obeying to command to one day transcend, neither master nor slave, even to yourself.

But none of this is easy. Daily you encounter possibility—and daily, duplicity. Danger. Disaster. You give in to things you know will harm you and give up passions when they get too hard. The deficit of gratification pushes you not onward but in tiresome circles. You deceive yourself. You willfully distract. With excuse after excuse you defend yourself when showing up late or not at all in your own life.

Granted, the world is scary—perilous and in peril. Social forces push you in uncomfortable places. Controlled political climates stifle and confound. You swear it's worse now than it was for your parents, and your children will damn you for the mess you'll leave behind.

But the conditions have not and will not change—nor has or will the presentation. But now more than any other Not Dead generation, you are aware of the presentation as a presentation—and you are sickened by the medium. The sleekness of the packaging. The slickness of the language. You understand the reasoning behind the machinery even if you disagree with it—but you cannot stop, escape or ignore it.

Not because prosperity or disaster is just around the corner. Prosperity and disaster are here.

The kingdoom has come.

The crisis is now.

Where do you turn for help? Professionals? Corpse pose? The people around you who are equally lost, if not the architects of your misery? Is "help" even a useful word, suggestive as it is that you don't get it?

You don't fit.

Though perceptions have changed, biology and bureaucracy have not. You are ill equipped mentally, emotionally and socially, and civic instruction has not kept pace. Skilled with detecting condescension and deceit, you must approach dilemma with a system of honest inquiry. You must strive for wellness not with the premise that you want to be better or to perform your best, but with the acknowledgment you are broken and just want to be good.

You want to be *okay* in this perpetual state of emergency. If you must wrestle—and you must—with truth and trust, artifice and agenda, the paranoia is founded and the trauma is real.

You want more than a series of attachments to and detachments from this world. You want understanding—and the assurance you'll be all right. You will. You always were. You are. The sharpest tool. The prettiest dying star. Both lock and key to all of life's mystery, misery, magic and dread.

You were past.

You will future.

Today, you are here.

And You Are Not Dead.

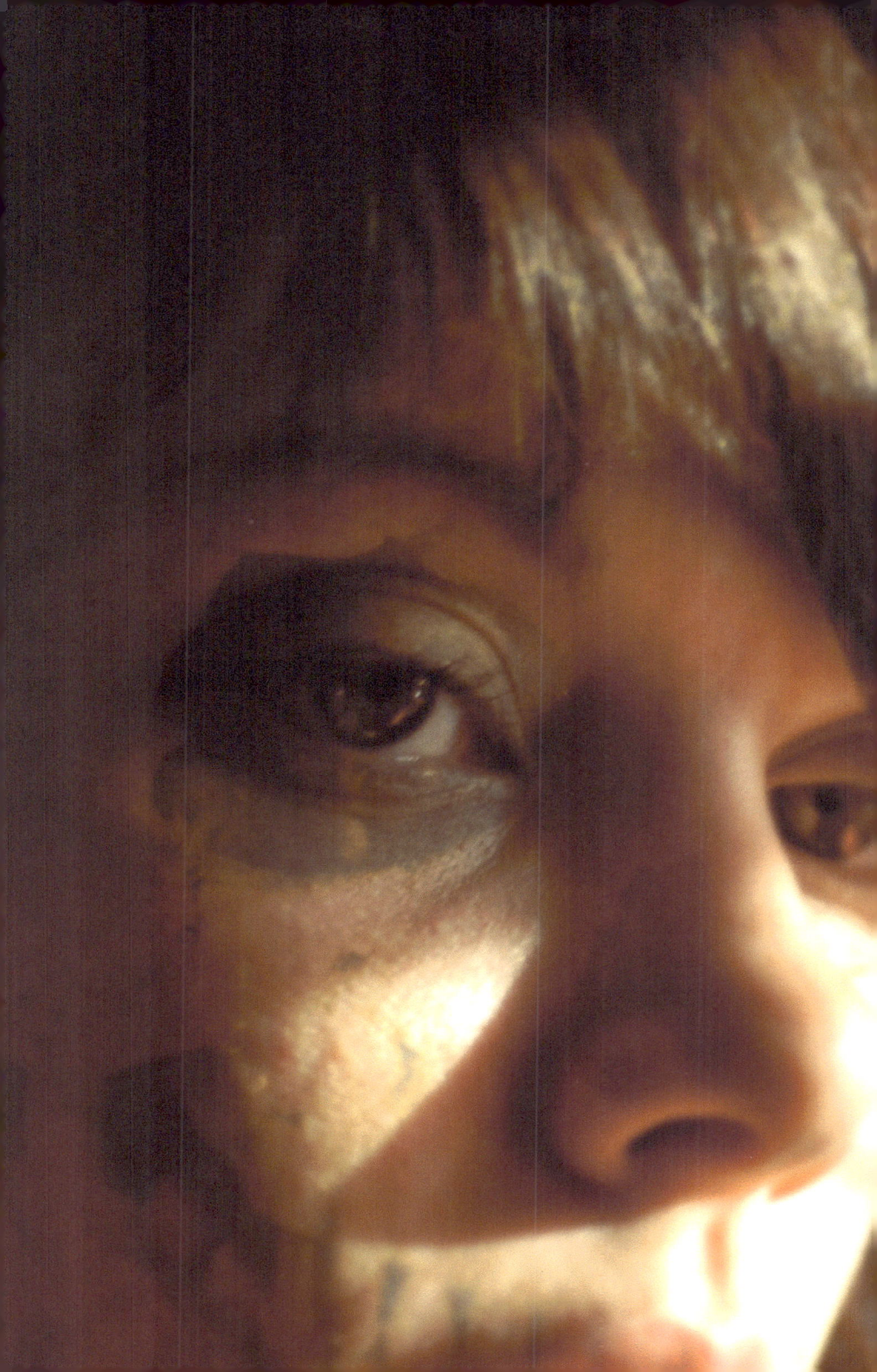

2. Where Do You See Yourself in Five Years?

Answer to yourself.

_____

_____

_____

_____

_____

_____

_____

_____

No, this is not a job interview or date interrogation.

This is only your life.

Maybe five years is not enough. Maybe five months, or minutes, will suffice. Or maybe you've reached the point where you don't think you can change—that growth and goals aren't important. Maybe you're right.

You're wrong. This question of projection that slows down and distresses so many in-the-moment modern thinkers is important. For five years or fifty, not having a confident answer does not make you devoid of goals, but it does indicate a lack of deference for mobility. A final destination dictates a direction and requisite course of action. Without it, you meander, and the awesome being you strive to become is never born.

You can't let this happen.

Your future life is waiting.

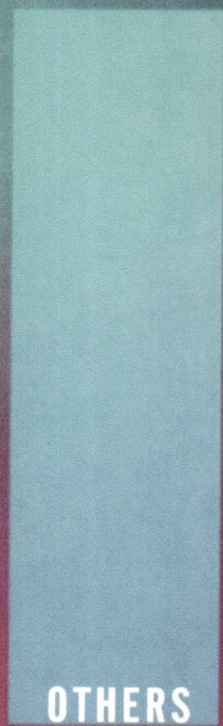

Not to say you aren't trying. Your accomplishments are many and admirable. But when you fall short, you tend to cut the wound deeper with sharp thoughts and self-deprecation. Ensnared in a cruel yet common expectation, you are pressured to succeed but not instructed how to do it. How do you proceed—and consistently thrive—when hearing the demand for ground-breaking scientists and death-killing doctors along with no less dedicated, no less fully actualized line cooks, custodians and parking attendants?

In order to meet—and surpass—expectations, you must first adopt them. Pay more attention than you produce, and don't be shy to sacrifice talent for stability. Hate your job? At least you're participating. Deciding between doing what you love and doing what is right is a difficult lesson to earn.

Even in poor economies, opportunities abound—the ones you take, and the ones you make. Concentrate on the surefire. Put on hold or choke the untenable. If something is meant to be, it will happen anyway. That's fate. You have to stay out of its way.

If you are the nervous type—always doing things—you may feel compelled to actively pursue the frivolous. This is acceptable only if you can gaurantee payoff. Demand-driven ventures are the targets you should strafe. They not only butter your bread, they eat it for you.

Do not chase personal projects fetid with hope. Stop nursing brainchildren foul with ambition. Know what people want, and give it to them.

Schemes may not be foolproof,

but dreams are proof of fools.

3. Five Years Ago, Did You See Yourself Here?

Explain yourself.

_____

_____

_____

This perhaps is the real question—the contemplation of where you thought you were going and where you have ended up. Five years ago. Fifteen. Your minutes of fame dutifully performed, downplayed and passed away. To see yourself in the future or to regard yourself in the now, you must track where you were and how it relates to your previous plans.

You did have plans, right? Even poor designs are better than none. Without a map to life, existence tempts death, lacking coherence and discernible milestones to indicate growth. Let's presume you had goals. Let's assume they were exceptional and, being realistic, unrealistic. The average person thinks he or she is above average. Aiming to achieve more than you're cut out for doesn't set you back, it keeps you right on track.

As such, however, a five-year assessment commonly requires you to adjust your ideals to suit your current motivation. If your accomplishments deserve congratulations, by all means, think highly of yourself. But do not bruise your ego if you know you have failed. In fact, you should reward failure if by recognizing oversight you regard yourself in a new light—a light that wants to be brighter.

Just don't claim disadvantage or conspiracy. Falling short is not your fault—nor is it anyone else's.

True or false:

_____ Falling short is not your fault.

_____ It is anyone else's.

Challenge truth or lie:

_____ Climbing high is not to your credit.

_____ The success of others wears off on you.

Life is a series of patterns. You wake up. You fall asleep. You seek attention. You horde glee. You succumb to wholesale delusion and death. You fall prey to emotional inefficiency. Determine what factors contributed to these patterns so you can replicate or avoid them. Be honest with yourself. Be cruel enough to force change.

What has been done to you that has proven productive?

_____

_____

_____

What have you done pale of progress and merit?

_____

_____

_____

What is wrong with you?

_____

_____

_____

_____

_____

_____

_____

_____

_____

_____

_____

_____

What is right with you?

_____

_____

What did you mean to change that instead changed you?

_____

_____

What is left of you that you're proud of?

_____

_____

What remains that you abhor?

_____

_____

_____

_____

Why are you like this, and why don't you care?

_____

_____

Remember: Even if you have been dead before,

You Are Not Dead now.

4. The Advantages of Becoming a Landowner

Have you ever said to others, or braver, to yourself, "Money's not important. It's just money." Perhaps you chose a lower-paying path because the scenery was nicer and the tasks, better matched. The spouse, more attractive or attached—with less expensive suits and shoes, but more stylish genes.

Face it. With basic wants to need, bills to pay, conveniences to lease and down payments to make, you need money. Divorcing yourself from the drive for financial stability dismisses reality and kills all hope of keeping a more than minimum level of comfort. You want a more than minium level of comfort, don't you?

☐ Yes.

It's okay to want things. It's okay to get them. *You're* okay when you give money the power to speak to and through desire. Be your voice when you buy your choice. Contribute to your identity—not through "things," but how you choose to spend money.

You're not a passive consumer. You're an active consumer. You vote with your dollars for the materials you enjoy and the modes of manufacturing that align with your values. You also shine true with your keen shopper savvy, hunting down bargains and capitalizing on discounts that allow you even more purchase.

Groceries, vehicles, clothing, appliances, vacations and nights on the town—all of these are meaningful transactions, but the greatest satisfaction comes from buying a lasting home. Renting is like throwing your money down a hole. Loaning lets your money dig for you—the key to long-term depth.

Though it may sound uncouth, nothing can compare to acquainting yourself with the soil of your own land—smelling the dirt and sensing the solid weight of the earth behind you. Owning property also provides shelter for your stuff. It establishes stability, a belonging of belonging. It restores the dignity the quest for money dissolves.

If money is the root of evil, we are the devil's sharecroppers.

Someday you will buy the farm.

5. Agents of Change

Which of the following has existed since time began?
  a. War.
  b. Poverty.
  c. Violence.
  d. Human misery.

The present day gives you in addition:
  a. The constant threat of other people's terrorism.
  b. Privatization.
  c. Job insecurity.
  d. Fear.
  e. Uncertainty.
  f. Doubt.

All of the above push you below.

More than you think is less than we know.

To not be depressed, you would have to be dead.

Argue all you want that society needs the fix—don't treat the symptoms, cure the disease. But you alone can't solve the world, and add to social stress the personally anguishing **(check the following)**:

- ☐ Misplaced love.

- ☐ Lingering aspiration.

- ☐ Feelings of worthlessness and alienation.

All increase tension and misunderstandings with coworkers, family and friends. But it is not a crime to feel anxious or hopeless. What is criminal is not trying to quit.

Perhaps you try self medication. Cold beer and whining. Hard spirits and soft spirituality. Strip joints and joints and all flavors of party favors topped with the glaze of blasé escape. Imprisoned behind Nanaimo bars. Beneath Tim's bits. You only indulge socially, you say—but the company of your demons doesn't count.

Alarmingly for many continuing a life of pain or decadent destruction appeals more—is safer—than confronting the social stigma of mood-improving agents such as Paxil, Xanax and Zoloft. Those who suffer are more concerned with insisting they're okay and normal than striving to *be* okay and normal. But what exactly is the stigma?—besides the phenomenon of disgrace for thinking and feeling to the point of despair.

Before acquiring an abstract meaning, stigmas referred to real-life bleeding—boils and lesions that riddled a body and indicated disease, which warded off the healthy for fear of contagion.

What do you and a leper with gaping holes have in common? What, precisely, is your stigma?

Surely not trying to help yourself feel better, think more clearly and act with poise. No—it's stumbling about with a sick heart and bleeding mind.

Put away those bad feelings.

Prevent those bad thoughts from happening.

You Are Not Dead.

Stop pretending that you are.

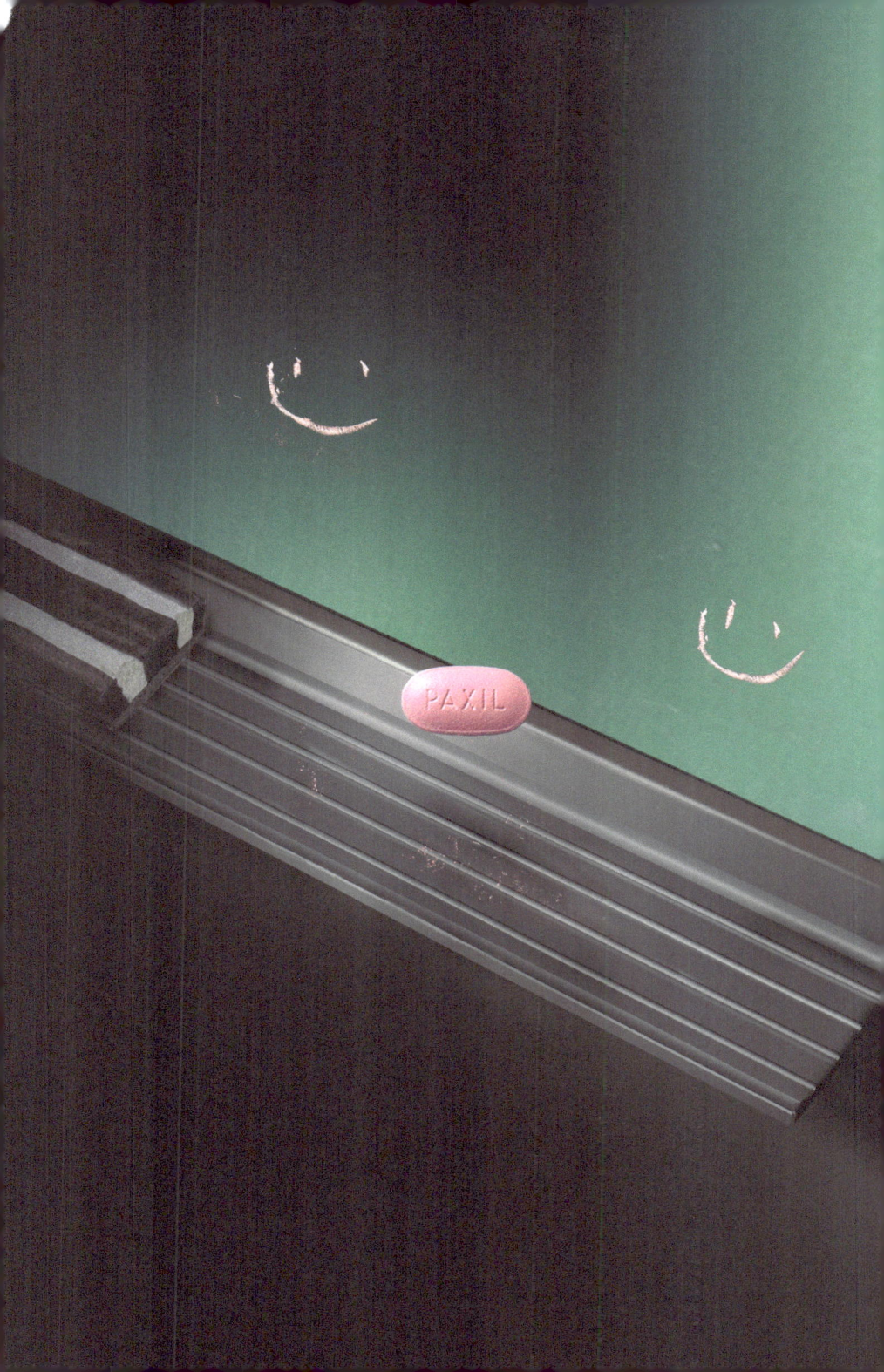

6. The Risks and Benefits of Mediacation

Life is distracting. Death has your full attention. Not Dead lies somewhere in between. Whether you can name more MPs than professional athletes or identify deeply with the reality on TV, diversions abound in everyday doing, and they can overwhelm.

Daily Not Dead requires escape, and television, newspapers, the internet and more provide ample outlet for media medication.

Consuming infotainment calms you down and cheers you up after unpleasant days at the office—not to mention hurries along the awkward hours between the end of the workday and bedtime. Being in the know also secures your inclusion in friendly conversation. If others must constantly fill you in, your not paying attention can jeopardize their favorable opinion of you.

There are risks, however, to media-induced nonstop good times and cultural attrition. What if your escape becomes the place you're always at? What if you need to escape your escape? What might that even look like?

Draw a picture on the next page.

Was this helpful?

☐ Somewhat.

☐ No.

Ambivalence is a common response to complicated forces. Media soothes and excites but also distracts, sometimes at the expense of what you think you should be accomplishing, even if that something is figuring out what it is.

If this is the case, change your media. If always watching a particular channel, give another one a try. Swap the TV for the YouTubes or pick up some movies from the video store. You may even read a magazine. At the first sign of irritation—unrest, fatigue or inordinately disorganized or absent thoughts ("the blahs")—switch it up. Experimentation will ensure a healthful balance.

If you are adventurous, exciting new trends can be found online where other people exactly like you construct unique identities and release creative energies for free. Discover what you're like and dislike. Become Not Dead in your Second Life. Rant and rate and vote up others' genius, contributing to collective greatness and force—you, a molecule of water in a massive wave, the thumb in the fist of a giant you helped create.

Media reveals so much about you. It forms and informs your attitudes and preferences, bedrocking your beliefs then backing them up with sponsored expertise and high-impact graphics.

This knowledge is not only power, it's proof:

It would be destructive and distasteful

not to want to know more about you.

7. Declaring Your Codependence

Knowing thyself is not just for personal reference. You need to learn who you are so you know how to act when someone special wants to get to know you, especially since, in the end—or for the little ends throughout your life—it's better if it's not you who knows you best.

Love is a many splintered thing. Dalliance, dating, seduction, rejection, all lead to elation or darkest woe. Perhaps you have been the target of a stray arrow. Worse, you may fall for someone who doesn't know you don't exist.

You may progress deep only to endure—or commit—equally deep transgressions, slashing hearts, shattering lives, abusing emotions and causing irreparable harm to one's capacity to trust ever again and/or cope with existence in general.

But after a thoughtful search for a combatable match—a trial of process, error and compromise—you may be inspired to profess significant otherness and make a declaration of codependence.

You follow the trends. You know the risks.* But that doesn't mean you shouldn't try to outwit statistics and imagine into reality full romancipation.

With your sweetmeat ever at your side, you benefit losing personal freedom. You hazard happiness and peace of mind as you share with your tolerated one your troubles and anxieties then feel them fall apart with the power of empathy or get demeaned to the point where you don't discuss them anymore. That's not so terrible, even for the selfish, and commitment isn't about increasing your burden by taking on another's, but exchanging support and helping each other achieve joy.

So exchange those vows. Give misery its company. Practice affection and positive reinforcement. Lives will get messy, but we all know one vacuum cleaner is cheaper than two. Besides:

There is nothing you can tell your heart to make it die.

*Past performance does not guarantee future results. Insufficient communication, less than satisfactory principle, faulty mutual trust and unforeseen maturity gaps may complicate the shared life investment—especially once the period of grace has elapsed. Even if the synergy with merging is at a premium, over time, endowments and overall performance will degrade—yours included. Additionally, merging assets for the production of yield may provide subsequent future securities. However, the initial investment is substantial and the outcome may not be favorable. Even the brilliant and well intentioned produce mean results.

8. Stop Identity Theft Before You Happen

You have been to soirees and other public spaces where, upon meeting someone new, after Hello drops the inevitable So What Do You Do? You may cringe when you hear this question, but it doesn't stop you from asking it yourself. How you make money and spend precious time defines your personality and social worth. You don't really care whether strangers enjoy what they do. You just need to know if they can help you.

The answer is Yes. If another's occupation or leisure time fixation intrigues you, Oh? How Did You Manage That? is an acceptable ruse for How Can I Become You?

People have several careers and professional distractions throughout their lives, but you can only pursue and fail so many. Find what works for others and adopt their behaviors. Therefore, yes, every interaction is a selfish maneuver. But it's also an exchange—mutually beneficial. Be a good resource. Enlighten others with dazzlement.

Only you know about...

    This funky restaurant: _____

    This free parking downtown: _____

Only you have the perspective of...

    This childhood trauma: _____

    Your secret dream: _____

Just as important as identity construction is identity preservation. Safeguard your Safeway card, your SIN, your pins, your electronic loonies, and use different passwords and security questions for all your online accounts.

If you elect to keep savings, far worse than having your good name tarnished, your time wasted or your assets drained is knowing thieves will be having more fun with your identity than you do.

They will get the biggest TV and the tiniest phones you've ever seen. They'll all have LASIK surgery then mountain bike the Andes, and buy the loft with the best view and optical wire everything. Can you imagine the humiliation of someone being better at being you than you? Confront the miser within. Become the thief yourself. Guarantee identity by indulging your desires.

Still keep your information safe.

Just don't keep much *in* the safe.

9. Debit to Society

This isn't just about identity. This is about our whole society, culture and conspicuous affairs with complex consumerism and economic catastrophe. No one can convince you that without exception the national deficit is good for the country. Knowing collective debt plunges deeper into the red makes you uneasy. If you can manage your expenses, why can't the government?

But maybe you can't balance your personal budget—and if you can, maybe you shouldn't. The economy is just like you. You want stimulation. You need security, and maintaining debt keeps you from getting lazy. You're also more likely to treat yourself when victories need rewarding.

Match the victory to the reward:

Having a job	Sofa
Having good taste	Vacation
Satisfaction	Fine wine

Wouldn't life be dull if luxuries were commonplace and the little things unnoticed? Just take care to strike a proper balance. Live too far beyond your means, and you're bankrupt. No more point to purchase points. No more climbing up.

One of the safer, more productive debits is the higher education loan. Rising tuition rates attest to institutional prestige and the importance of even the most impotent degrees. If you're not nervous about finding gainful employment, you're not paying enough. Aim high—fly high.

If you have already completed university, keep this in mind for your freeloading children, your derelict grandchildren and especially for yourself. Careers disappear, and you will need to retrain to keep abreast with overseas workers and emerging technologies.

But don't settle for getting fired—get fired up. Torch outdated ideas about dignity, repurpose your purpose, return to school then rise from the soot a well-rounded phoenix. Burned, perhaps, but with multiple degrees.

It takes money to make money. It takes money to fake money. Interest rates may be high, but who would want to be less interesting? Just as hardy savings entice theft and threaten your identity, debt indicates you take your life seriously—you hold the reins and control your destiny.

So build up debt like a tower to heaven.

With each expense, loan, debit, degree and intention,

you'll not only reach for the stars, you'll grab them.

TO WHOM IT MAY CONCERN

10. Note to Self Delusion

Throughout history, lasting contributions in science and mathematics, even philosophy, are due to notions of utter lunacy. What farfetched and fantastic idea isn't considered chimera until the moment it becomes reality? At the level of the individual, however, overloaded with unfocused desire, implausible dreams impede personal growth, suffocating as they offer hope.

Does the object of affectation notice you notice?

☐ Yes.

☐ No.

Will that novel ever write itself?

☐ Someday.

☐ No.

Will you have the good manners to deflect praise when recognized at last for your brilliance?

☐ Yes.

Delusions offer transport and deliverance, prospects more appealing in theory than fact. You worship the door but fear to turn the knob. You pay no mind to the fraud behind the curtain—everything is too flawlessly flawed. You have perfected feeling like shit. To let go of that kills the one thing you're good at.

LIFE

Delusions have become the events in your history, the signposts, the points of demarcation—before this falsehood, after this fantasy, making the timeline of your life a lie. Wishes you need to come true. Past slights you feel hobble you. Faith in other people's bigotries to excuse your failure to thrive.

Investing energy in keeping these delusions alive distracts you from creating real events in your life: ones not confined to your ingenious but fractured mind.

You accommodate the farce and accept the deception as a part of who you are. And it is a part of who you are. But is it a part of who you want to be?

Explain.

_____

_____

_____

Delusions are injuries you insist on having. Stop hurting. Demand healing. And if you think your delusions are risks worth taking, then confront them right now—not when you feel ready. Not when you think nobody's looking, everybody's looking at themselves. And if they are looking at you, they're tired of looking at you. They are sickened by what they see.

Take a chance. Leap.

You'll feel better eventually.

11. The Path of Least Existence

You've made it this far—in the *Guide to Modern Living* and in life. You want to go further: dream bigger, soar higher, worry less and succeed more. But you also just want to get by.

Stand on guard for thee... but not get dirty.

Be judicious but not judge. Act in your best interests.

Raise a fist and run.

How do you know what's important? What's authentic? What's safe? What is worth your effort, involvement and stress, and what is best left for someone else to fix?

Many believe that desiring is deserving. The more you want it, the more you should have it. When you fail, it isn't because you didn't work hard enough. You didn't *want* hard enough—and not just for personal gain. You know the world owes you nothing. Instead you are in debt to all of its trappings and want to give back more than trash and poison.

You want to conquer corruption—to raise aloft the downtrodden. But given the magnitude of problems, results will not satisfy, and the integrity of your intent will be under attack. You can never do enough, and what you do accomplish is complicated by your privilege that thinks it can determine what constitutes improvement.

It is devastating to realize you lack sufficient want. It's too damn confusing to not desire at all. You deserve what you get. But you don't always get what you deserve—and often, that is best.

Let the craving to aspire, accomplish and become be an end in itself. Need want but regard actually getting as dangerous and empty. The middling way guarantees stability. The path of least existence will keep you safe.

Above all, don't confuse dissatisfaction with complacency. Don't believe dissonance means you're doing something wrong. Thinking yourself progressive, a reasonably good person, but knowing the depth of your indifference, helplessness and apathy—this is still progress. It's perfectly reasonable, and still reasonably good.

Lack of fulfillment doesn't fragment experience.

Experience fragments experience.

And you want to be whole.

YOU ARE NOT DEAD!

Well, it's true. And through repeated perusal of this guide, your awareness and understanding of better living through not dying will increase and exhume: all doubt, all dark thoughts, all frail dreams.

As you continue your journey with your new ideas, you may slip into old habits or unhelpful thoughts. Don't curse these transgressions or fault yourself. The only shortcoming you could possibly commit is denying you too contribute to prosperity—you have a place in and duty to disaster. Find comfort within crisis and how you choose to deal with it. Turn trauma into triumph and a blind eye to blame.

Do your part. Feel all right. Witness your improvement and allow it to delight, exhilarate and calm. You're okay. Okay?

☐ Okay.

Never give up giving in to feeling it. Allow it to consume.

Being Not Dead, as glorious as it is, will be over soon.

YOU'RE WELCOME.

www.ingramcontent.com/pod-product-compliance
Lightning Source LLC
LaVergne TN
LVHW010016070426
835511LV00001B/1